外　滩

历史和变迁

主　编：楼荣敏
副主编：吴　成

上海画报出版社

THE BUND

HISTORY AND VICISSITUDES

Editor-in-chief: Lou Rongmin
Deputy Editor-in-chief: Wu Cheng

SHANGHAI PICTORIAL PUBLISHING HOUSE

主　编：楼荣敏
副主编：吴　成
编　委：马晶华　纪振英
　　　　吴光华　程绣明
翻　译：陈锡镖

Editor-in-chief: Lou Rongmin
Deputy Editor-in-chief: Wu Cheng
Members of Editorial Committee:
Ma Jinghua   Ji Zhenying
Wu Guanghua   Cheng Xiuming
Translator: Chen Xibiao

光荣增斗志　　屈辱励雄心

——《外滩》画册序

唐　振　常

　　尽管上海被颁定为历史文化名城,但它不是古城旧都,上海历史重在近代。唯其历史短,历史文化遗迹旧址便多较完整。上海之大,何处可以为历史文化之代表? 有人从青浦地下发掘去找上海人的根,史前出事何足为人文历史之据? 即使以今上海的建制上溯,昔日人文荟萃之邦的松江、嘉定,亦属古代的辉煌,渺乎远矣。老城厢应是近现代上海华界奋起的根据地,然今日之老城厢旧迹渐泯。南京路只是真正的珠光宝气了,珠光宝气非即昔日上海的实貌。淮海中路则大失昔日的宁静和风格,非夫旧观。写这么几句话,并非主张一成不变。变而不失其固有风格,在今天上海,似成一难事。

　　值得高兴的是,今日上海还巍然有一个外滩在。外滩亦有变,但是,变而不失其体,旧址完整保存,新颜乃在盛饰其巍峨,渲染其景观,增添其协调统一的气氛,外滩仍然是外滩,然是改革开放条件下观外滩,是历史之旧而人事之新。如此,以外滩作为上海的代表,是恰当的,外滩当之无愧。

　　近代上海,从外滩开始走向繁荣,走向世界。当年,背负屈辱的城下之盟,上海道台宫慕久指定了这一荒凉之地给随枪炮而来的英国人居住,谁曾想到,历一百年而有了远东第一大都会的现代上海。租界的产生,主权的丧失,是颟顸无能又无现代外交知识和主权意志的清政府所不明白,亦夫是侵略者挟其淫威逐步谋得。上海的发展有一过程。外滩从始至终经历了全过程。洋行之设,银行之建,海关之迁入,领馆之建立,外报之始创,公园之开辟,皆始于外滩,延及于其周围地区,外滩是上海近代历史的见证。

　　以上所举诸端,于沟通中西,于上海的发展变化,皆具历史的意义。然考其实质,对上海和上海人民来说,则光荣与屈辱二义均在焉。光荣者,上海能以宽大的胸怀,容纳“非我族类”的先进的物质与精神的设施和内涵,并吸取其意识,进而华界奋起直追,一改旧观,开全国文明建设之先声。而对于外来的租界统治者不合理地强加于上海的种种屈辱,上海人民的爱国斗争此起彼伏,载于史册,这更是上海的光荣了。屈辱者,洋行初以贩卖鸦片毒害上海和全国人民为务,外资银行则掌握上海的金融命脉,领馆则溢出其职权,与租界当局左右其势,任意妄为,外报则反客为主,颠倒黑白,公园则"华人不得入内"。为是等等,上海以斗争化屈辱,励奋其志,事有大成。上海之成其为上海,上海之力,上海人之力也。

我们说要尊重历史,保存历史。尊重历史者,尊重历史之真实也;保存历史者,保存历史之真相也。唯如此,方能从历史中求经验教训,所谓鉴往知来便是。不真,其识必偏,其经验教训就是对历史的误释,不足为训。几年之前,建立了外滩历史纪念馆,通过文献图录,于外滩的历史有可信的说明,使游览外滩者得于建筑本身所不备或阙失的历史文化,有深切的领会,用意即在保存历史真实,以励来兹。纪念馆设在外滩公园内,我视之为还兼有对历史的弥补或匡失之义。这个公园诚然并非了不起的佳构,然它是上海的第一个公园,也是中国的第一个公园,与前此满布全国的私家园林相对言,一个公字,文化意义迥然有别,它为上海社会注入了市民意识,这是近代上海大异于全国之所在,所以值得纪念而不宜废也。而纪念馆图录所载昔日外滩公园"华人不得入内"引起的上海人民的斗争,也正说明了屈辱励雄心的事实。

外滩历史纪念馆以其所藏,编为《外滩》画册出版,在近年已出版的各种画册中另存一格,我以为可见光荣增斗志、屈辱励雄心之意,乐为作序如上。

The Glory Heightens Morale, the Humiliation Encourages Aspiration

——An Introduction to the Picture Album "The Bund"

Tang Zhenchang

Although Shanghai is promulgated as a famous city with rich historical and cultural traditions, yet it is not an ancient city or old capital. The priority of its history lies in the modern age. Only because of the short history, its historical and cultural relics and former sites are comparatively well preserved. Since Shanghai is such a large city, what can be the representative of its history and culture? Some people try to look for the roots of Shanghai people from the unearthed cultural relics in Qingpu County, but how could the prehistoric legacy be the foundation of its humanistic history? Even if dating back to the time when the magistracy was set up in Shanghai, the former towns of gathering talents such as Songjiang and Jiading belonged to the ancient splendor, which have little influence nowadays. The old town of Shanghai should be the base area in which the Chinese area of modern Shanghai rose vigorously, but the old town site of Shanghai is gradually diminishing today. Nanjing Road is now really adorned with brilliant and glittering jewelry, yet the brilliance and glittering was not the real image of old Shanghai. Huaihai Zhong Road has now been deprived of its peace and characteristics of the old days, so that its old appearances no longer exist. What I am writing here does not mean that I advocate to be fettered by the traditions. What I idealize is the development without losing its innate characteristics, which, in today's Shanghai, seems difficult to de satisfied.

Fortunately, the Bund is still existing majestically in today's Shanghai. Although great changes have taken place on the Bund, yet its mainstay remains unaltered, its old site is completely preserved, and new scenes are added to its grand magnificence from time to time, applying new colors to its scenery and increasing the atmosphere of its integrated and harmonized unity. The essence of the Bund is still there. To observe it in the view of the age of reformation and open–door in China, I think the Bund not only remains its historical characteristics, but also is beautified by the later generations of Shanghai people. Therefore, it is appropriate to take the Bund as the representative of Shanghai, and it deserves.

Modern Shanghai began to be prosperous and go to the world arena from the Bund. Under the humiliated and forced agreement in the 1840s, Kong Mu–jiu, the Shanghai taotai designated this bleak and desolate land for the residence of British who came here with guns and·cannons. Who can imagine that Shanghai became the first metropolis in the Far East only after one hundred years? Because of the muddle–headed and perfunctory Qing government which knew little about the contemporary diplomatic knowledge and sovereign determination, or because the aggressors plundered with the abused power, foreign leased territories began to emerge, and China's sovereign rights lost gradually. There has been a process of Shanghai's development, and the Bund experienced the whole process from the beginning. The Bund witnessed the modern history of Shanghai, during which foreign hongs were established, banks founded, Customs moved in, consulates set up, foreign newspapers issued and parks opened up. All these events originated on the Bund, and thereby extended to nearby areas.

What mentioned above has profound historical significance both to the connection of China with western countries and to the development and transformation of Shanghai. But examining its essence closely, we find that these events mean both glory and humiliation to Shanghai and Shanghai people. The glory is that Shanghai assimilated "foreign" advanced material and spiritual institutions and connotations, and absorbed its consciousness, so that the Chinese areas in Shanghai rose up vigorously. As a result, the old appearance was changed and the civilization construction was pioneered in China. For the various humiliations forced upon Shanghai by the governors of foreign leased territories, the patriotic struggles of Shanghai people took place one after another which were recorded in the history. Shanghai is really proud of these heroic records. What disgraced Shanghai is that the foreign hongs in Shanghai firstly took the selling of opium as their major trade to poison Shanghai people as well as the people in the whole country. Foreign owned banks controlled China's financial lifelines, and foreign consulates abused their powers to influence China's political affairs and did whatever they wanted to do. Foreign newspapers played the major roles in China's media, and always turned matters upside down. Parks were not allowed "admission of Chinese", etc. Shanghai people dispersed these humiliations by unyieldingly struggles, and their determinations were encouraged and the great achievements were made at last. Shanghai is becoming today's Shanghai with Shanghai's strength, and the strength of Shanghai people.

It is often said history should be respected and preserved. To respect history is to respect the historical realities, and to preserve history is to preserve the true historical image. Only in this way, can the experiences and lessons be sought out from the history. It is what we say to foresee the future by viewing the past. If the history is distorted, its comprehension must be biased, and the lessons and experiences must be the misunderstanding of the history, therefore, there will be no instruct which can be drawn from. Several years ago, the Bund History Museum was established. Through documents and documentary pictures, the history of the Bund is expounded in a credible way, so that the tourists to the Bund can further understand the historical culture beyond its buildings. It is intended to preserve the historical reality, so as to encourage the future generations. That the memorial hall is set up in the Bund Park, I think, has the meaning to remedy and rectify its history. This park, of course, is not an outstanding piece of construction, but it is the first park in Shanghai as well as in China. Compared to those private gardens suffusing previously among the country, the cultural connotation of the word "public" is entirely different, it injects the awareness of citizenship into Shanghai and that makes Shanghai greatly different from the other parts of China. Therefore, it is worthy of being commemorated instead of being discarded, and in those days the notice of "Chinese are not allowed to enter" recorded in the documentary of the memorial hall gave rise to the struggles of the Shanghai people. It also proves the humiliation encourages aspiration.

The historical objects remained in the memorial hall are compiled into the picture album "The Bund" and to be published. It has the unique characteristics among the various picture albums published in recent years, the tenet of which, I think, is that the glory heightens morale, and the humiliation encourages aspiration. Therefore, I am pleased to write this introduction.

目　　录

CONTENTS

开　　埠

　　上海的开埠是英帝国主义大炮轰开的,鸦片战争以后,上海被迫对外开埠。根据中英《南京条约》,上海于1843年11月17日开埠,英人(首先是外交官、商人和传教士)陆续来到上海租地发展。

The Opening of the Port

　　Shanghai Port was forced to open by the British Imperialists armed with cannon. In accordance with the provisions of the Sino–British Nanking Treaty signed after the First Opium War, Shanghai began to be an open port on November 17, 1843. The British (firstly, diplomats, merchants and missionaries) came to Shanghai in succession to lease land for development.

19世纪的外滩
The Bund in the 19th century.

《南京条约》签字场面

The scene of signing "The Nanking Treaty"

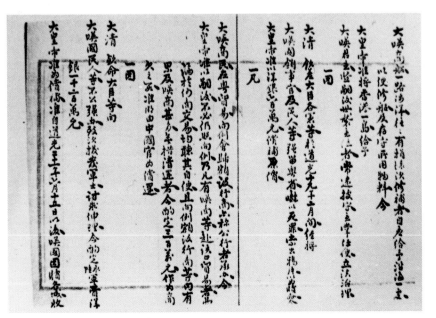

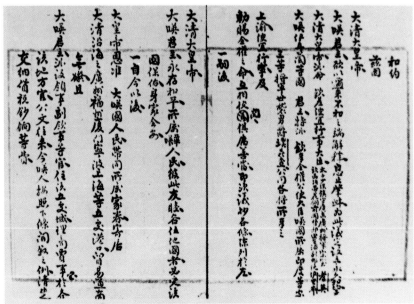

《南京条约》抄本

The transcript of "The Nanking Treaty"

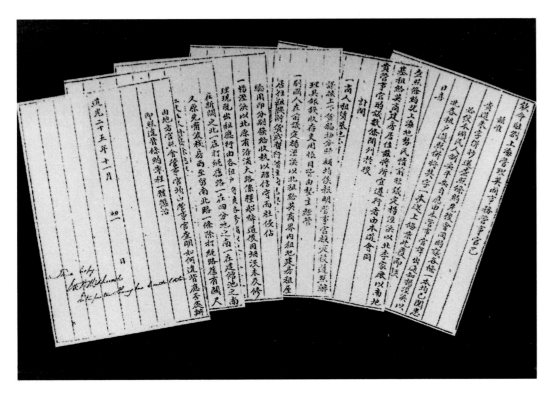

1845年，英领事巴富尔与上海道台宫慕久订立《租地章程》（复印件，原件存英国国家档案馆）。

In 1845, British Consul Balfour and Shanghai Taotai Kong Mujiu signed the first "Land Regulations" (This is a copy of the original, and the original is stored in the British National Archives).

上海开埠公告

The proclamation of
opening Shanghai Port

was "impracticable for 50 or more ships to swing." The passage left on the Pootung side for junks, of which from two to three thousand lay above, varied in width from six to eight hundred feet, from which it will be seen that the extreme width of the river off the Bund was then about 800 yards. It was considered "inconvenient" for ships to anchor below the Soochow Creek limit.

No immediate delimitation of the settlement was made except that the river was to mark its eastern, and the Yangkingpang its southern boundary. The west was left entirely undefined, while on the north, what is now the Peking Road was the first boundary, the land lying to the north of that being at the time partly Government land, and partly what was known as the Li Chia Chang, or Li family enclosure, all of which for awhile was considered as outside the settlement limits. As a whole the settlement site was of the usual local type. The main portions of it were fairly well raised and cultivated; others were lower, and some seem to have been quite waste. There were numerous creeks, ditches, and ponds, and the lower grounds were in summer time covered with reeds. Population was scanty. For some years after the first comers arrived, men considered themselves "in the country" once they had got west of what is now the Szechuen Road. The Bund was a towing path and little more, with a foreshore many yards wide uncovered and covered as the tide ebbed and flowed.

The first formal notification by Capt. Balfour of the establishment of a Consulate is dated the 14th November, 1843, and opens thus, "I hereby notify to all Her Majesty's subjects that I have temporarily established the British Consulate within the City of Shanghai in a street situated close to the walls between the East and West Gates." He goes on to declare the port open for trade on the 17th inst. from which date all treaty regulations would be in force. Ships were to anchor head and stern if necessary, and a later rule ordered that no shifting of anchorage was to be done without permission of the Commander of the British man-of-war. The six "partners" in the "Shroff Shop" were entitled to grant receipts for export and import duties and tonnage dues. Consular fees for reporting and clearing ships were fixed at $5, but this was shortly after reduced to $1. A very early attempt was made to introduce a Bonding system, but the Imperial Commissioner was opposed to the scheme and nothing came of it.

It was the day of small things so far as trade was concerned, but it is not without interest to note that during the first six weeks after the port was opened, that is to say, from 17th November, to 31st December, seven vessels entered. Their average capacity was 281 tons, and the average number of their crews 25. The largest ship was the "Eliza Stewart" of 423 tons, and the smallest the

洋　行

1843年起，英、美等国纷纷在上海设立从事贸易的洋行，到1854年，洋行已达120家。

Foreign Hongs (Foreign Firms)

From the year of 1843, Great Britain, the United States and other countries kept pouring into Shanghai to establish foreign hongs to engage in trade. By 1854, there had been about 120 foreign hongs in Shanghai.

19世纪50年代的外滩
The Bund in the 1850s.

外滩鳞次栉比的洋行

Foreign hongs lined along the Bund.

美商旗昌洋行

Russell & Co., Ltd. (American).

英商沙逊洋行

David Sassoon & Co., Ltd. (British).

英商怡和洋行

Jardine, Matheson & Co., Ltd. (British).

19世纪80年代的外滩北眺和南望

The northern and southern views
of the Bund in the 1880s.

鸦片交易

早期的洋行几乎无一不与罪恶的鸦片交易有关,他们输入鸦片,输出金、银、丝、茶,随着鸦片从士绅普及到民众,滚滚白银流入英国等国手中。

19世纪60年代以后,由于海内外正义舆论的谴责,以及西方资本主义对华贸易政策的变化,上海的外国洋行从主要贩卖鸦片,转向从事杂货和机制棉纺织品的贸易。

The Opium Trade

Nearly all the foreign hongs in early days engaged in evil opium trade. They exported opium to China, and took gold, silver, silk and tea to their home countries. With the habit of smoking opium spreading from the gentry to ordinary people, more and more silver *yuan* was taken away from China by Great Britain and other countries.

After the 1860s, under the condemnation of just public opinions as well as the changes in the trade policy of western capitalist countries toward China, foreign hongs in Shanghai began to take up groceries and cotton textile products instead of opium as their major trading commodities.

黄浦江上怡和洋行的鸦片船
The opium ships of Jardine, Matheson & Co., Ltd on the Huangpu River.

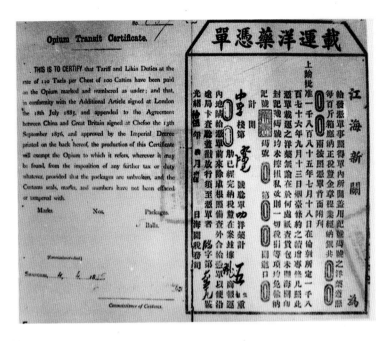

洋药(鸦片)凭单

The voucher of the foreign drugs (opium).

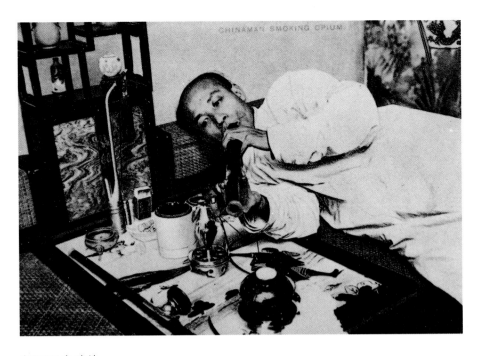

市民吸食鸦片

City residents smoking opium.

码头上待输出的茶叶

Tea piled on the wharf to

be exported.

丝绸出口

Silk export

租　　界

英国首任驻沪领事巴富尔凭借不平等条约，要求上海道台将上海以北临江的一块土地划给外国人租地建房。经过两年的谈判，1845年划定洋泾浜（今延安东路）以北、李家宅（今北京东路）以南为外国人居留地。这就是最初的租界。

The Settlements of Shanghai

Based on the unequal treaties, Balfour, the first British Consul in Shanghai, asked Shanghai Taotai for a piece of land along the River and to the north of Shanghai City for foreigners to lease and build houses. After two years' negotiation, an area was designated for foreigners to reside. Its location was from the north of Yang–King–Pang (now Eastern Yan'an Road) to the south of Li–Ka–Za (now Eastern Beijing Road). This was the first leased land in Shanghai.

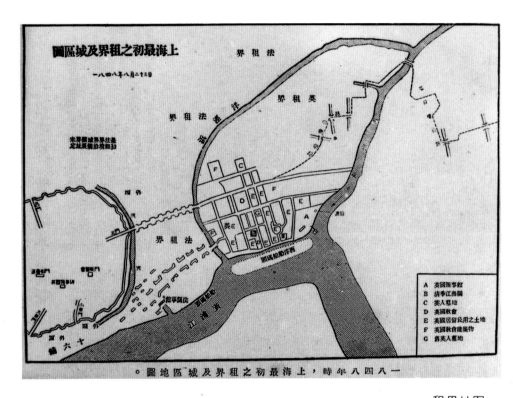

租界地图

An map of the settements.

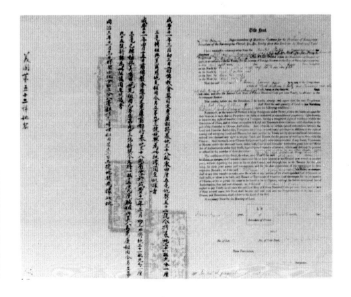

租地道契

Two Title Deeds.

首任法国驻沪领事敏体尼1848年1月23日履任，年底就迫使清政府同意设立法租界。

Montigny, the first French Consul in Shanghai, took office on January 23, 1848. By the end of that year, he had forced the Qing Government to establish the French Concession.

租界界碑

The boundary stone.

游弋于黄浦江上的外国军舰是租界的强大依靠，图为帝国主义侵华武装（英海军陆战队）。

The foreign fleets cruising on the Huangpu River were the powerful backing of the foreign settlements, The photo shows imperialists' armed aggressive forces in Shanghai (British marine corps).

侵华列强在检阅军队。

Aggressive great powers in Shanghai inspecting troops.

美军兵舰侵驻上海黄浦江。

Aggressive American fleets stationed on the Huangpu River.

美国圣公会传教士文惠廉是上海美租界
的创始人。

William Jones Boone, the missionary of American Church Mission was the founder of Shanghai American Settlement.

英、美、法三国领事没有得到清政府的许可,就联合修订和签署了第二个
《土地章程》。

The Consuls of three Powers, Great Britain, the United State and France revised and
Signed jointly the second "Land Ragulations", without Qing Government's permis-
sions.

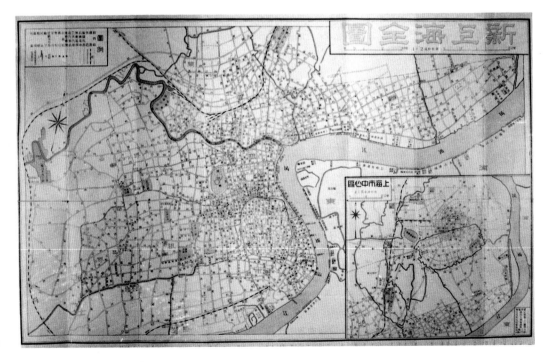

租界扩张图

The map of the Settlement's expantion.

租界的管理

租界原是外商居住、经商之地。由于清政府腐败无能，外国人不仅日益扩张租界的范围，而且攫取了界内的立法、行政、司法等中国主权，使之成为国中之国。

The Administration of the Settlements

Originally, "settlements" were places of residence and business for foreign merchants. Due to the corruption and ineptitude of the Qing Government, foreigners had not only been able to expand the settlements, but also seized the legislative, administrative and judicial sovereignty of China, so that it became "a state inside of the state"

工 部 局

1854年7月，英、美、法等国成立统一管理租界的市政机关工部局，工部局设有商团、警务处、卫生处、工务处、学育处、公共图书馆、音乐队、华文处等办事机关。

Shanghai Municipal Council

In July, 1854, Gread Britain, the United States, France and other countries established the municipal administrative organization to govern the settlements comprehensively, in which many offices were set up, such as Volunteer Corps, Police Departmant, Public Health Department, Public Works Department, Education Department, Library, Orchestra and Band, Chinese Studies etc..

1854年建立的工部局就是这位英国领事阿礼国的"杰作"之一。

Shanghai Municipal Council founded in 1854, was one of the "masterpieces" of the British Consul, Alcock.

公共租界工部局的最高决策机构为董事会，图为工部局董事合影。

The council was the policy-making of S.M.C..this is a group Photo of the members of S.M.

总董座椅

The chair of Chairman of the
Council.

建于1913年的工部局大厦,位于福州路、江西路。

The Municipal Council Building was completed in 1913, which was situated at the corner of Foochow Road and Kiangse Road.

工部局局旗(现藏于上海市档案馆)

The flag of S.M.C. (It is preserved in
Shanghai Municipal Archives).

工部局印章(现藏于上海市档案馆)

The seal of S.M.C. (It is preserved in
Shanghai Municipal Archives).

法租界公董局的徽记
The seal of the French
Concession Council.

1862年,法租界脱离工部局管辖,成立了自己的行政机关——公董局,独立管理法租界。图为建于公馆马路(今金陵东路)的公董局。

In 1862, the French Concession separated itself from the juris diction of the Municipal Council, and established its own administrative institution to control the French Concession independently. The photo shows the French Concession Council on Rue du Consulats (now Eastern Jinling Road).

会审公廨

会审公堂制度始于1869年，会审公廨是中国政府设立在租界里的一个中外混合型司法机关，主审官由中国官员担任，租界内华人的案件由主审官直接处理，华洋之间的纠葛由外方参与会审、陪审或听诉，因此中外之间不同的司法体系也常常在这里发生冲突。

The Mixed Court

The system of the Mixed Court began in 1869, and it was a Sino-foreign mix-up judicial organization in the Settlements. The magistretes were Chinese officials, who heard the cases between Chinese people in the Settlements directly. The trials of the disputes between Chinese and foreigners were participated by foreign assessers in the form of joint hearing, serving on jury or trying sitting in the audience. Therefore, differences between the judicial systems of China and foreign countries often conflicted in the Mixed Court.

1899年搬到洋泾浜边上的会审公廨。

The Mixed Court that was moved to the bank of Yang-King-Pang in 1899.

1880年位于南京路的会审公廨。

The Mixed Court situated on Nanking Road in 1880.

审理犯人时，外国领事既可参与"会审"，更可接受上诉。

While hearing the case of criminals, foreign consuls did not only participate in "joint hearing", but also accepted appeals.

在印度巡捕监押下做苦工的会审公廨犯人。

The prisoners of the Mixed Court were doing hard labour under the supervision of Sikh constables.

海 关

上海辟为商埠以后,海关税务是一项重要的财源。1854年,上海道台在北门外头坝南面浦设立了一个关署。1853年9月小刀会起义捣毁了关址。英国驻沪领事建议将收税机关建在租界内,并且以外国人管理,当时清政府为急于得到税款应付财政,就同意了此建议。

The Customs House

Since Shanghai became an open port, customs duties had been an important source of revenue. Shanghai Taotai established a customs office at the Southern Douba outside the North City Gate. In September, 1853, the office was demolished in the uprising of the "Small Sword Society". The British Consul in Shanghai proposed that the customs fouse was established in the Settlements, and controlled by foreigners. The Qing Government approved the suggestion in order to get customs duties to balance its revenue and expenditure.

清咸丰十年(1857年)设立于外滩的江海北关

The Imperial Maritime Customs House was established on the Bund in the 10th year of Hsian-Feng (1857).

1893年改造后的江海关

The Shanghai Customs House after the rebuilding in 1893.

1927年，新海关大楼落成。

The new Customs House Building completed in 1927.

英国人赫德，曾担任中国海关总税务司48年，实际控制了中国海关，并且将西方现代海关管理制度引入中国。

Robert Hart, an Englishman, had been the Customs Commissioner General in the Customs of China for 48 years, and in fact he dominated the Customs House of China in the period. He also introduced the modern system of customs administration into China.

座落于海关门口的赫德铜像

The bronze statue of Robert Hart at the entrance of the Customs House.

租界武装

1853年，小刀会在上海起义，美、英等国以"保卫租界安全"为借口组织了义勇队（后称万国商团）。1870年以后，商团移交工部局指挥，成为工部局直接控制的租界常备武装，以保证租界的行政独立。

The Army of the Settlements

In 1853, under the pretext of protecting the security of the settlements, Great Britain and the United States, etc. organized the Contingent of Volunteers (Later called Shanghai Volunteer Corps). After 1870, Shanghai Volunteer Corps was handed over to the Municipal Council, and became the standing army in the Settlements under the direct control of the Municipal Council on purpose to guarantee the independent administration in the Settlements.

万国商团轻骑队
The Light Horse Company of Shanghai Volunteer Corps.

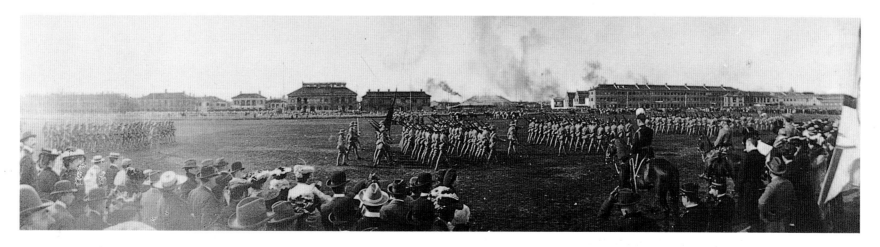

操练中的万国商团士兵

The soldiers of Shanghai Volunteer Corps were training

万国商团的徽记
The insignia of Shanghai Volunteer Corps.

1905年，上海总商会在租界筹组了华人义勇队——华商体操会，1907年该会加入工部局万国商团成为中华队。图为中华队在操练。

In 1905, Shanghai Commerce Chamber organized the Chinese Volunteer Corps—the Athletic Association of Chinese Merchants in the Settlements. In 1907, it joined Shanghai Volunteer Corps and became the Chinese Company of it. The photo shows the Chinese Company at drill.

巡　捕

上海自元代设县以后，就设置了县尉和巡检司，这两个衙门的职责就是"巡捕"——维持地方治安。当外国人把西方Police Man引入上海时，上海人将它译成"巡捕"。

The Police Force

When Shanghai became a "Xian (county)" in Yuan Dynasty, it set up two offices—Xian Wei (a police department) and Xun Jian Si (an inspecting department). The duties of these two departments were to "Xunpu" — to keep peace and good order. When foreigners introduced western policemen into Shanghai, they were called "Xunpu" by Shanghai people.

公共租界工部局中央捕房
The Central Police Station of S.M.C.of
the International Settlement.

1929年加层以后的法租界中央捕房
The storey-added building of the Central Police
Station of the French Concession in 1929.

工部局西捕
An Foreigh constable of S.M.C.

工部局华捕
The Chinese constables of S.M.C.

工部局印捕
The Sikh constables of S.M.C.

公董局越捕
The Vietnamese constables of the French Concession.

法租界总巡捕房徽记
The insignia of the Central Police Station of the French Concession.

搜身——俗称"抄把子"
Frisking—it was called "Chaobazi" in Shanghai slang.

25

领 事 馆

外滩是上海最初的租界，1846年英国首先将设在上海县内的领事馆迁到外滩后，各国也纷纷在外滩设立驻沪领事馆。

Consulates

The Bund was the first settlement in Shanghai. In 1846, Great Britain moved its consulate from Shanghai City to the Bund, and after that, other countries also established their consulates on the Bund in succession.

英国领事馆：1843年11月英国首先在上海县域內设立领事馆，1846年迁到外滩，图为1873年建成后的英领事馆。

The British Consulate: In November, 1843, Great Britain firstly established its consulate in Shanghai City, and then moved it to the Bund in 1846. The photo shows the British Consulate completed in 1873.

美国领事馆：1846年美国驻沪代理领事华尔考脱在旧纤道(今九江路)设立美国驻沪领事馆。

The American Consulate: In 1846, Wolcott, the American Deputy Consul in Shanghai, established the American Consulate in Shanghai on Rope Road (now Jiujiang Road).

法国领事馆：1848年1月法国驻沪领事敏体尼在洋泾浜租赵方济主教的住宅设立法领馆，图为1895年建于公馆马路（金陵路外滩）的法国领事馆。

The French Consulate: In January, 1848, Montiginy, the French Consul, leased Bishop Francois Xavier Marescu's residence at Yang-King-Pang to establish the French Consulate in Shanghai. The photo shows the French Counsulate completed in 1895 on Rue de Consulats (at the corner of the Bund and Jinling Road).

德国领事馆：1852年德国将领事馆设于黄浦路，1937年迁至北京路外滩。

The German Consulate: The Germany established its consulate on Huangpu Road in 1852, and moved to Peking Road near the Bund in 1937.

市政建设

　　为了适应城市经济和自身活动需要,租界当局一开始就按照西方现代化模式来经营管理租界,使道路、桥梁、公共交通、邮政、电讯及供水供电等基础设施和公用事业逐步完善,到19世纪末期,华界也以租界近代市政的模式加以改造,大规模的市政建设为上海城市的现代化提供了条件。

The Municipal Construction

　　In order to meet the needs of city economic and social activities, the Municipal Authorities administered the Settlements in accordance with the modern western model from the very beginning, and gradually perfected the infrastructure and public utilities such as roads, bridges, public traffic, postal service, telecommunication, water supply, power supply and so on. By the end of the 19th century, the Chinese controlled areas were also rebuilt step by step according to the modern model of municipal administration in the Settlements. Large scale municipal constructions laid the foundation for the modernization of Shanghai.

1864年英商上海自来火房(煤气)诞生。1865年,上海在中国最早建立煤气公司,图为19世纪80年代建于苏州河畔的大型钢结构的煤气罐。

In 1864, Shanghai Gas Co.,Ltd. was founded. In 1865, China's first gas company was founded in Shanghai. The photo shows the huge steel-structured gas tank built near the bank of Soochow Creek in the 1880s.

1865年上海最早的一盏街头"自来火灯",因其管道由地下而出,沪人称之为"地火"。

The earliest "gas light" in Shanghai appeared in 1865. Because its pipelines came out under the ground, so it was also called "ground fire" by Shanghai people.

1871年外商上海大北电报公司设立的海线与香港接通,上海开始有了与国际通讯的先进手段。图为大北电报公司。

In 1871, the Great Northern Telegraph Co., Ltd. a foreign corporation in Shanghai, laid a marine cable to connect Shanghai with Hong Kong. Therefore, Shanghai had the advanced means of international communication. The photo shows the Great Northern Telegraph Co., Ltd..

大北电报公司发报间

The telegraphy room of the Great Northern Telegraph Co., Ltd..

1881年上海出现了电话，1882年外滩建成第一个"德律风"公司电话亭。

In 1881, Shanghai was equipped with telephone, and in 1882, the first telephone booth of Shanghai Mutual Telephone Co., Ltd. was built on the Bund.

电话接线
Telephone wiring

1892年工部局收回商办的上海电力公司，在斐伦路(今九龙路)建起新发电厂。

In 1892, the Municipal Council took over the privately-owned the Shanghai Power Company, and established a new power plant on Fearon Road (now Jiulong Road).

这是发电厂高达120英尺的大烟囱。

This was the big chimney of the power plant with the height of 120 feet.

1887年花园桥上已高悬"夜明珠"般的电灯,桥西两侧的煤气灯却未"退役",两者并存,交相辉映。

In 1887, electric lights were already hung up like "night pearls" on the Garden Bridge, but the gas lights on both sides to the west of the bridge were still "in service". Both of them existed side by side, enhancing each other's beauty.

1882年上海在中国最早建立自来水公司,图为江西路自来水公司办事处及侧旁的自来水塔。

In 1882, China's first water company was founded in Shanghai. The photo shows the water tower beside the office of the Shanghai Water Works Co. on Kiangsi Road.

水陆交通的发展，促进了上海近代邮政事业兴起，1875年上海海关附设寄信官局，1896年大清邮局设立于上海。

The development of water and land communication promoted the rise of modern postal service in Shanghai. In 1875, Shanghi Customs House set up an attached post office. In 1896, the Imperial Post Office was established in Shanghai.

1880年工部局在租界內主要干道构筑地下排水管。

In 1880, the Municipal Council constructed the drainage
systems under the main roads inside the Settlement.

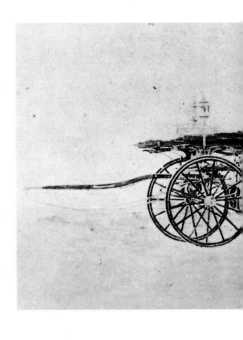

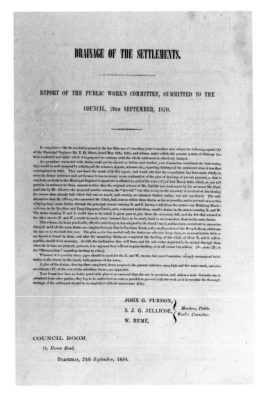

工部局工务委员会和工部局工程师奥利弗(E. H.
Oliver)于1870年向董事会提交《租界的排水设施》
报告。

The member of the Public Work's Committee of S.M.C. and
the Municipal Engineer E.H.Oliver submitted the report on
"Drainage of the Settlements" to the Council in 1870.

太平军兴起时,租界当局为防止战火损失,于同治二年(1863年)向美国购置救火机一具。

During the Tai-Ping Uprising, the Settlement's authorities, in order to prevent the losses from the warfare, purchased a fire engine from the United States in the second year of Tong-Zi (1863).

相隔不到10年租界内有了蒸汽救火车,在当时属十分先进的消防设备。

In no more than ten years, steam fire engines appeared in the Settlement, and the fire-fighting equipment was quite advanced at that time.

同治五年(1867年)租界的救火会(消防队)宣告成立。图为1885年12月扑灭福州路大火后的救火队员。

In the fifth year of Tong-zi (1867), it was proclaimed to establish the Fire Brigade in the Settlement. The photo shows the firemen after put out the great fire on Foochow Road in December, 1885.

1880年前后的洋泾浜，河道日渐淤塞。

Yang-King-Pang around 1880. Its river
course was gradually silted up.

洋泾浜上最靠外滩的一座桥——外洋泾桥。

Outer Yang-King Bridge——the Bridge over
Yang-King-Pang close to the Bund.

洋泾浜填浜前埋下巨大的排水
管。

Huge sewers were embedded underground before Yang-King-Pang was filled up.

昔日洋泾浜为英、法、华三界的交界处,
1914年6月11日起被填平。

Yang-King-Pang which used to be the junction of the British Settlement, the French Concession and the Chinese Areas was filled up in June, 1914.

铺设电车轨道。

Laying Tramway track.

铺设南京路。

Paving Nanking Road.

已铺设完成的铁藜木路面。

Jarrah wood blocks paved on
road surfaces.

1901年匈牙利人李恩斯携两辆汽车来沪,这是上海街头最早的汽车。

In 1901, Leanse, a Hungarian, took two motor cars to China. These were the earliest cars in the streets of Shanghai.

1908年3月5日,第一辆有轨电车出现在马路上。

On March 5, 1908, the first tramway ran on the roads of Shanghai.

1914年11月,第一辆无轨电车出现在马路上。

In November, 1914, the first trolleybus ran on the roads of shanghai.

1924年10月9日上海有了第一辆公共汽车。

On October 9, 1924, Shanghai possessed the first bus.

南京路上行驶的双层巴士。

The double-deck bus running

on Nanking Road.

20年代中期，敞顶的双层巴士成为沪上交通新景观。

In the mid of the 1920s, open double-deck buses became a

new scene in Shanghai's traffic.

1856年建造的韦尔斯吊桥。
Wells' Drawbridge built in 1856.

1873年建成的花园桥,又称白渡桥。
The Garden Bridge was built in 1873, and it was also called "the Public Bridge (Free Ferry Bridge)."

1907年建成的钢桁架外白渡桥。

The beam-structured Public Bridge was completed in 1907.

1908年外白渡桥上已行有轨电车。

The tramcars were passing over the Public Bridge in 1908.

连接浦江两岸的载人交通工具长期以竹篙、浆橹为"动力",这种木船的"一统天下"既费时,又危险。

For a long period of time, wooden boats were the means of communication which carried passengers across the Huangpu River. These boats, driven by bamboo poles and oars, were not only slow, but also dangerous.

有着统一编号的摆渡舢板。
The numbered sampans crossing the River.

1910年由"浦东塘工局"为"便利办公起见"租了一条小机轮,拖上三只木船,附载过江旅客,结束了黄浦江无轮渡的局面。

In 1910, "the Dyke Engineering Bureau of Pudong", in order to facilitate their work, leased a steam boat towing three wooden boats to carry their employees and other passengers to and fro the Huangpu River, ending the situation that there was no steam boat ferry on the Huangpu River.

1928年上海特别市政府开办了第一条公共对江航线。

In 1928, the first public ferry route was opened by Shanghai Special City Government.

往返于黄浦江两边的小贩。

Hawkers to and fro the Huangpu River

南京路铜人码头
Bronze Statue Wharf
of Nanking Road.

市渡轮开往浦东东昌路

十六铺码头

China Navigation

Co. Wharf (the 16[th]Pu Wharf).

北京路双层浮码头外观

The outward appearance of the double-decked pontoon of Peking Road.

北京路双层浮码头鸟瞰

The bird's-eye view of the double-decked pontoon of Peking Road.

本世纪20年代的外滩南望

The southern views on the Bund in the 1920s.

本世纪20年代的外滩北眺

The northern views on the Bund in the 1920s.

东方华尔街

外滩是上海开埠后最早开发完成的黄金地段，其位置显赫，地价昂贵，在这块寸金之地拥有房地产、设置办公楼，标志了实力和信誉，所以很多外资银行都不惜代价挤入外滩，谋求发展。当时外滩周围聚集了各国颇具实力的银行。正当各国银行为确立其在外滩的地位而展开激烈较量之计，1897年中国第一家华资银行中国通商银行在外滩开业。1905年中国第一家国家银行清户部银行也在外滩开业，尤其是1928年之后，四行（中央银行、中国银行、交通银行、农民银行）二局（邮政储金汇业局、中央信托局）的总部均设在上海，上海已成为全国的金融中心和远东的金融中心，而这个中心的位置就在外滩一带。

The Wall Street of the Orient

The Bund was the first developed golden section after Shanghai had become an open port. Its location was so eminent and land prices were so high that it was a symbol of strength and prestige to own real estates and set up offices on this piece of land, where an inch of land was worth a thousand pieces of gold. Therefore, many foreign banks tried their best and spared no cost to acquire some room on the Bund for the sake of development and prosperity. At that time, many foreign banks with huge assets were gathered around the Bund. While the banks of various countries were competing fiercely to establish their statues on the Bund, Commercial Bank of China, the first Chinese capital Bank, was opened for business on the Bund in 1897. In 1905, Ta-Ching Government Bank, the first national bank in China started business on the Bund. Especially after 1928, four banks (Central Bank of China, Bank of China, Bank of Communications, Agricultural Bank of China) and two bureaus (Postal Remittances and Savings Bank and Central Trust of China) set up their headquarters in Shanghai. By that time, Shanghai had become the financial center in China as well as in the Far East, and the Bund was the core of this center.

1847年，英国丽如银行在上海开设分行，成为第一家进入中国的外资银行。

In 1847, Oriental Bank Corporation of Great Britain established a branch in Shanghai. It was the first foreign bank in China.

1857年宣告成立的英国麦加银行上海分行。
The Shanghai Branch of Chartered Bank of India, Australia and China of Great Britain was established in 1857.

1865年筹建的汇丰银行成为以后数十年外国资本控制中国金融势力的最重要堡垒，图为1874年建的第二代汇丰。

Hong Kong and Shanghai Banking Corporation was proposed to establish in 1865, which, in the following several decades, became the most important stronghold of foreign capitals to control China's finance. The photo shows the second office building of Hong Kong and Shanghai Banking Corporation completed in 1874.

1861年设立的英国的有利银行上海分行。
The Shanghai Branch of Mercantile Bank of India of Great Britain was established in 1861.

第三代汇丰银行大厦耗资1000万元,图为建造中的汇丰银行大厦。

The third office building of Hong Kong and Shanghai Banking Corproation cost ten million yuan. The photo shows the office building of Hong Kong and Shanghai Banking Corporation under construction.

1923年6月落成的汇丰银行大厦气势宏伟。

The Hong Kong and Shanghai Banking Corporation office building completed in June, 1923, looked magnificent and imposing.

1890年，德国设立于外滩的德华银行。

Deutsch-Asiatische Bank was set up by Germany on the Bund in 1890.

1899年，日本设立于外滩的台湾银行。

Bank of Taiwan was set up by Japan on the Bund in 1899.

1893年，日本设立于外滩的横滨正金银行。

Yokohama Specie Bank was set up by Japan on the Bund in 1893.

中国第一家华资银行由盛宣怀发起，官商合办的中国通商银行于1897年7月诞生在黄浦江畔。

The first Chinese capital bank was Commercial Bank of China initiated by Sheng Xuanhuai and jointly owned by the government and merchants, which was opened on the Bund in July, 1897.

各国银行纷纷进入上海，上海已成为国际商埠。为了便于各种货币兑换、流通，马路边、街道口都设有换洋钱的亭子。

Because the banks of various countries were established in Shanghai in succession, Shanghai became an international commercial port. For the convenience of the exchange and circulation of different currencies, booths of exchanging foreign currencies were set up along the roadsides and at the street corners.

华俄道胜银行是中国第一家中外合资银行，总行设在俄国的圣彼得堡，上海分行于1896年在外滩开业。

Russo-Chinese Bank was the first Chinese-foreign jointly owned bank in China. Its headquarters was situated in St. Petersburg in Russia, and Shanghai Branch started business on the Bund in 1896.

具有国家银行性质的户部银行上海分行，1905年设于外滩，1908年改称大清银行，1911年民国后改称中国银行。

The Shanghai Branch of Ta-Ching Government Bank, which was a national bank in nature, was set up on the Bund in 1905. Its name was changed to Ta-Ching Bank in 1908 and then to Bank of China in 1911 when China became a republic.

1908年设于外滩的交通银行，兼有国家银行与专业银行的性质。

Bank of Communication was set up on the Bund in 1908, and it had the nature of a national bank as well as a specialized bank.

上海第一家综合性交易所——上海证券物品交易所（1920年7月1日开业）。

The first comprehensive exchange in Shanghai—Shanghai Security and Goods Exchange started business on July 1, 1920.

远东中心

经过多年发展,外滩的汇丰银行是上海和远东的金融领袖;汇中饭店、沙逊大厦是亚洲最豪华的饭店;《字林西报》是东方西侨的言论喉舌;上海总会里有世界上最长的酒吧;怡和洋行掌握着中国大部分进出口业务;太古轮船公司主管着东亚大部分的航运;气象台是亚洲的中心台……总之,外滩每一座大楼都汇聚了中国乃至远东的各种信息,成为东方总枢纽。

The Center of the Far East

After many years' development, Hong Kong and Shanghai Banking Corporation became the financial leader in Shanghai and the Far East. Palace Hotel and Sassoon House were the most luxurious hotels in Asia.《North China Daily News 》was the mouthpiece of public opinions among the western residents in the East. The bar in Shanghai Club was the longest one in the world. Jardin, Matheson & Co., Ltd. controlled China's most import and export business. Butterfield and Swire Co., Ltd. was in charge of the major part of shipping business in East Asia. The Observatary was the central Observatary in Asia. In short, various information from China and even from the Far East was assembled in each building on the Bund and the Bund became the general pivot in the East.

汇中饭店
The Palace Hotel.

沙逊大厦
The Sassoon Building.

《字林西报》
《North China Daily News》.

《字林西报》大楼
The building of 《North China Daily News》.

外滩天文台
The Astronomical Observatory on the Bund.

太古轮船公司
Butterfield and Swire Co., Ltd.

上海总会(一期、二期）
Shanghai Club (the First phase
of the building, the second phase
of the building).

本世纪20年代中期的外滩

The Bund in the mid of the 20th century.

冒险家的乐园

　　上海开埠后,旧时的荒滩逐渐变成了洋场,不少外国的冒险家来到上海,他们有的来时两手空空,一转眼就腰缠万贯,变为富翁。十里洋场的南京路及其起点的外滩变成了冒险家的乐园。

The Paradise of the Adventurers

After Shanghai had become an open port, the uncultivated lands in the old time was gradually turned into metropolis full of foreign adventurers. When they arrived in Shanghai, they were very poor, but in an instant, they became very rich, turning out a man of wealth. Nanking Road which was called ten-*li* metropolis and its starting point—the Bund was turned into the paradise of adventurers.

哈同,犹太人,从鸦片贸易中积聚最初资本后,就转向投机房地产业,牟取暴利。1931年6月,哈同病逝后,留下土地460余亩,各种房屋1300多幢,上海南京路上著名的四大公司,其中永安公司、新新公司的地皮都属哈同所有。

Hartoon, a Jew, accumulated initial capitals in opium trade, and then turned to invest in real estate to make exorbitant profits. After Hartoon died in June, 1931, he left more than 460 *mu* land and 1300 various houses. There were four famous companies on Nanking Road, in which the land of The wing On Co., Ltd. and Sun Sun Co., Ltd. belonged to him.

维克多·沙逊，沙逊第三代主持人。
Victor Sassoon, the host of the third
generation of the Sassoons.

沙逊投机房地产业成为上海第一房地产大王，他的产业除沙逊
大厦外，还有都城大厦、汉弥尔登大厦、华懋公寓、河滨大楼等。
Sassoon speculated on real estate and became the magnate of the real
estate in Shanghai. In addition to Sassoon Building, he also owned Me-
trope Hotel, Hamilton Building, Cathay Hotel, and Embarkment Building,
etc..

外国人花园

英租界划定后不久，租界当局将黄浦江、苏州河汇合处的一块新生土地修成"公家花园"，这是上海第一个外国人花园。1868年8月8日，外滩公园建成开放，不许中国人入内游览。

The Garden for Foreigners

Not long before the demarcation of the British settlement, the settlement authorities built a "Public Garden" on a piece of new land at the junction of the Huangpu River and Soochow Creek. This is the first garden for foreigners. On August 8, 1868, the Puflic Park was completed and opened, but Chinese were not allowed to enter and visit the Park.

公园全景
The panorama of the Park.

公园大门口

The gate of the Park.

公园音乐亭

The music stard of the park.

公园园规

The rules and regulations of the Park.

PUBLIC AND RESERVE GARDENS. REGULATIONS.

1. The Gardens are reserved for the Foreign Community.
2. The Gardens are opened daily to the public from 6 a. m. and will be closed half an hour after midnight.
3. No persons are admitted unless respectably dressed.
4. Dogs and bicycles are not admitted.
5. Perambulators must be confined to the paths.
6. Birdnesting, plucking flowers, climbing trees or damaging the trees, shrubs, or grass is strictly prohibited; visitors and others in charge of children are requested to aid in preventing such mischief.
7. No person is allowed within the band stand enclosure.
8. Amahs in charge of children are not permitted to occupy the seats and chairs during band performances.
9. Children unaccompanied by foreigners are not allowed in Reserve Garden.
10. The police have instructions to enforce these regulations.

By Order,
N. O. Liddell,
Secretary.
Council Room, Shanghai, Sept. 13th. 1917.

外滩新生

1949年5月27日，中国人民解放军解放了上海，上海人民欢欣鼓舞迎接解放，这也标志着外滩的新生。

The Rebirth of the Bund

On May 27, 1949, the Chinese People's Liberation Army liberated Shanghai. Shanghai people greeted the liberation with exultation. This marked the rebirth of the Bund.

上海解放仪式
The ceremony of Shanghai's liberation.

解放军进城露宿街头，与民秋毫无犯。

When the People's Liberation Army arrived in Shanghai, the soldiers spent the night in the streets, and the slightest violation of the people's interests was forbidden.

各界人民迎接解放
People from all walks greeted the liberation.

外滩庆祝国庆五周4. 大游行
Celebration of the 5th anniversary of
the National Day of the P.R.China.

国庆彩车
The floats of the National Day.

庆祝国庆十周年外滩夜景
Celebration of 10thanniversary of the
National Day of the P.R.China.

本世纪50年代起，西方各国在营造现代化高楼时，陆续拆毁了大量近代建筑，而风格迥异、造型独特的外滩建筑羣却完整保留下来。图为50年代外滩。

From the 1950s, while the contemporary buildings were being constructed in western countries, many modern buildings were demolished gradually. But on the Bund, many buildings with different characteristics and patterns were totally preserved. The photo shows the Bund in the 1950s.

外滩综合改造

随着国民经济的不断发展,处于市区交通蜂腰边缘的外滩已愈来愈显露出她的拥挤和众多的难堪。上海市政工程设计院的设计人员独具匠心地提出岸线外移的设计方案,增加了陆域面积,解决了拓宽马路、增加绿化、布置景点方面的需要。

The Comprehensive Remolding of the Bund

With the continuous development of the national economy, the Bund which is situated on the edge of traffic bottlenecked parts became more and more congested and manifested many problems. The designers of Shanghai Municipal Engineering Designing and Researching Institution put forward a plan with great originality. They proposed to move the shoreline outwardly, so as to increase the land areas and meet the needs of broadening roads, increasing green areas, arranging scenes, etc..

建造管桩支承空廊长廊防汛墙。

The construcfion of the suspended corridor and wall of flood prevention supported by pipe piles.

改造好的江堤，成为
外滩一大景观。

The remolded dike has
become a grand scene
on the Bund.

外滩灯光

1989年黄浦区人民政府决定用灯光来辉映外滩建筑优美绝伦的风姿,灯光工程采用冷光照明工艺,以不同的光色、亮度、角度照射建筑物,取得总体观赏的效果。

The Lighting of the Bund

In 1989, Huangpu District Government decided to enhance the exquisite charm of the buildings on the Bund. Luminescence lighting technology was adopted in the lighting engineering to light up buildings with different colours, luminosity and from different angles so as to achieve the effect of comprehensive view of the Bund.

走向新世纪的外滩

  上海市人民政府决定在黄浦江两岸规划建设上海的中央商务区,由浦东的陆家嘴金融贸易区和浦西外滩地区组成。经过几年努力,浦江两岸同时勃兴,外滩正以崭新的面貌走向21世纪。

The Bund Heads for the New Century

  Shanghai Municipal Government designed to build Shanghai Central Business District (CBD) on both sides of the Huangpu River, constituted by Lu Jia Zhui Financing and Trading District in Pudong and the Bund district in Puxi. After several years' efforts, both sides of the Huangpu River are prosperous at the same time. The Bund is going into the 21st century with new appearances.

74

封面题字：邓　明
责任编辑：杨秉良
　　　　　杨顺泰
装帧设计：梁　兵
Inscription: Deng Ming
Executive Editors: Yang Bingliang
　　　　　　　　　Yang Shuntai
Art Designer: Liang Bing

外　滩
历 史 和 变 迁

上海画报出版社出版
（上海长乐路 672 弄 33 号）
新华书店上海发行所发行
中华印刷厂制版印刷
开本 787×1092 1/12 印张 8 印数 0001－3000
1998 年 6 月第 1 版 1998 年 6 月第 1 次印刷
ISBN 7－80530－418－1
J·419　定价：精 70 元平 55 元